Never Never Never Will She Stop Loving You

The Adoption Love Story of Angel Annie

Revised Edition

by Jolene Durrant
illustrated by Adopted Children
photography by Steve Allred

JoBiz! Books at JoBiz!, Inc.
PO Box 910456
St. George, UT 84791
435-674-0056
www.birth-mom.com

This book is available through bookstores and internet sites.
Multiple copy discounts to agencies, support groups, etc. are available through the publisher.
Visit our web site, birth-mom.com, for updates on JoBiz! products and publications.
For information regarding speaking engagements, call 435 674-0056.

Publisher's Cataloging-in-Publication
(Provided by Quality Books, Inc.)

Durrant, Jolene.
    Never never never will she stop loving you : the adoption love story of Angel
Annie / by Jolene Durrant ; illustrated by adopted children ; photography by Steve Allred.
–Rev. ed.
      p. cm.
    SUMMARY: True story of a young woman called Annie, who cared for her unborn
child and placed him for adoption only because it was best for him; with a preface for
adults, including adoptive parents, birth parents, and the general public.
    Preassigned LCCN: 99-72088
    ISBN: 0-9663567-9-9

    1. Adoption–Juvenile literature. 2. Birthmothers–Juvenile literature. 3. Adopted
children–Juvenile literature. 4. Adoption. I. Allred, Steve H., 1952 II. Title.

HV875.D87 1999   362.7'34
              QBI99-1052

Printed in the United States of America

Hundreds of people have spoken with me about this story, its impact on their lives, and adoption in general since the original book was published last year. I appreciate all those who shared a part of their hearts with me. My understanding of adoption issues increased, and I began presenting information at support groups and conventions. Because of the overwhelming response to my conference presentations, I've chosen to summarize my message in this preface. Following these notes, the book appears in its original form. If this book is a gift for someone (child, birth mother, etc.), a page has been provided to write "a message just for you."

I invite all readers to pay special attention to the dedication page at the end of the book.

Jolene

No Spilt Milk

No little hands
That I can hold
No bedtime stories
That must be told
No skinned knees
No tears to dry
No spilt milk
Over this–I'll cry.

–Jolene Durrant (1979)

Notes to Readers

When we adopted our first child I felt like a hero. Opening our hearts and home to a child in need seemed pretty noble. Friends and family commented on how wonderful we were.

Then a birth mother, Annie, came to live with us, and I learned the real heroes of adoption are the birth mothers. In fact, birth mothers became more than heroes to me–they became angels. I needed Annie to stay with us to open my eyes. Now I invite you to open yours. I invite you into the heart of a birth mother.

Often adopted children have questions about the birth mother's love because they need specific details, like those found in this book. Feeling cared for, valued, and loved by their birth mothers can help adoptees learn to care for, value, and love themselves. Wise adoptive parents will bless the lives of their children with such information.

Placing a child for adoption is usually an act of great courage, responsibility, and love. Few people today realize this basic truth. As the adoption community and society reach out to understand, appreciate, and honor birth mothers and fathers, I believe more adoptions will take place.

How can the public support the adoption process and birth mothers in particular?

If you learn someone is a birth mother, ask her about her experience. Most want and need to share their stories. Use sensitivity and kindness in your choice of questions. In a birth mother support meeting one young girl stated, "Today one of my friends said, 'Do you ever think about your baby?' It hurt because it's more like, 'Do I ever not think about my baby?'"

Most birth mothers, whether they placed their baby last week or 30 years ago, would appreciate questions such as:

What's it like for you when people ask you if you ever miss your baby?
How do you deal with the pain of questions like that?
What conditions led you to place your child for adoption?
Is your adoption an open or closed adoption, and how satisfied are you with
  your level of contact with your child and the family?
If there is one thing you could tell your child, what would it be?
What questions do you wish people would ask you?
What moments would you want to experience with your child?
What types of things do you wish you could tell the parents who adopted your
  child?
When have you felt the most misunderstood as a birth mother?

These questions can be adapted for conversations with adoptees, adoptive parents, or birth fathers.

Notes to Birth Mothers (and Fathers)

Bless you for your courageous decision to place the baby you have nourished and cared for and held so close to your heart with parents that you feel are better prepared to meet the needs of a growing child. Out of your love and concern for your baby, you set aside your own motherly needs and desires.

From you, birth mothers, I have learned two profound lessons. It usually takes more love to place a child for adoption than it does to keep a child. And, there is not a greater mortal love than the love of a birth mother.

I feel very fortunate to have met so many of you. Your stories of love, strength, and commitment inspire me. To you and to the birth fathers who are committed to their children, I invite you to pay special attention to the dedication page in the back of the book. Many birth parents and their families find comfort in its message.

I encourage you to personalize this book by placing a label over Annie's name and putting your name in its place throughout the book. Also, change or add any details that fit your pregnancy–how you sacrificed for your child. Add as many concrete, specific details as you can. Make it real for your child.

Notes to Adoptive Parents

Like many of you, I wondered, "What if talking about my child's birth mother makes them love the birth mother more than me?" Along with many other adoptive parents, I've learned that sharing details about birth parents to an adopted child usually brings the child and adoptive parents closer together because the child usually feels comforted and relieved. Many also feel they are more whole because they have more information about their biological and possibly cultural heritages.

I choose to believe that if my children develop friendships and relationships with their birth parents someday, perhaps it will be because I have effectively guided them in loving and understanding many people.

No matter how loving adoptive parents are, most adoptees feel a sense of loss–loss of identity, culture, and connections to their past. The adoptive parents are their children's interpreters of loss. Children rely on parents to help them make sense out of major events as well as daily experiences.

How you view your child's adoption will have a lot to do with the adjustment the child makes in your family and the community. Not talking about adoption usually leads the child to the belief, "It's so bad they won't tell me about my birth parents." Too much talk and the child could feel the parents think the child needs protection, is defective, etc. Or they may suspect a dark secret that doesn't exist. One adopted teen told me she likes it when her parents answer questions as casually as she asks them. She doesn't need someone holding her hand and going into long conversations about simple questions, but some questions do need more intimate and lengthy discussions.

Because many children believe they can be no better than the parents to which they were born, one of the best possible gifts adoptive parents can give their child is guidance in believing they came from parents (at least a birth mom) who in some way cared about that child and his or her future. Hopefully there are many loving details and hopefully you will find ways to share them.

Happy stories about the excitement of the adoptive couple are wonderful but they don't answer the child's natural question, "Why didn't my birth mother keep me?"

After several months of single parenting, one teenage birth mother courageously placed her child for adoption. She had taken good care of her child, but became aware her child needed more than she could provide physically, emotionally, and educationally. Hopefully the adoptive parents have helped that child to appreciate the care the birth mother did give, have helped the child respect her for her wisdom and sacrifice, and have shared with the child how hard it must have been to have gotten to know and love the child and then still place the child out of concern for the child.

If little is known about the birth parents because the child was abandoned, don't assume the parents did not love the child. In some countries, birth mothers face possible imprisonment for bearing children. Fetuses are often aborted and girl babies killed at birth. Giving birth and then abandoning the child is the greatest act of love possible. We will never know how many mothers hide in the shadows and tearfully wait for their precious babies to be found, hopefully to be taken to orphanages where they will go to adoptive parents who will love them as much as these courageous birth mothers do.

And what of mothers who remain addicted to drugs and whose babies are born addicted? Or mothers who neglect their children, so that the children are taken by the state and placed for adoption? Could it be the mothers are deliberately but unconsciously making poor choices to insure the children go to better care–the better care they don't have the willpower or courage to provide any other way?

Bottom line. Give the child as many facts on his/her adoption that are known, are age appropriate for the child, and there is a purpose in sharing the information with the child. Ask yourself, "What is my purpose in sharing this information?", "Is my child ready for this information?", "Am I ready to answer some of the possible questions my child might ask?". Be sure it is in the best interest of the child to have the information and be prepared to help frame the facts in a positive light. If you are fearful about discussing adoption with your child, seek help from other adoptive parents, support groups, therapists, or adoption agencies. Your child's future happiness can be enhanced by the sharing of specific details. By sharing information about the birth parents, you can actually become closer to your child as you give your child the comfort and peace they don't have the words to ask for.

A Message Just for You...

Never
Never
Never
Will She Stop
Loving You

Jolene Durrant

Illustrated by Adopted Children

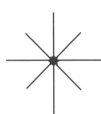

Dear Reader,

    If you are an adopted child you will probably like this book.

    I don't know your story, but I can tell you the story of Annie and her baby.

    It might give you ideas about your own birth mother and her love for you.

Self-Portraits of Children Artists

Dear Annie's Child,
You are a special boy,
because you have
two mothers.

One mother takes you to the park.

She makes you peanut butter
sandwiches.

And says,

"Get your homework done."

"Eat your vegetables."

And...

"I'm so glad you are my son."

This mom kisses you good night.

She will always love you.

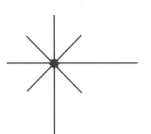

You have another mother.

She is your birth mother
and her name is Annie.

Annie will always love you.
  You might think,
    "She loves me?
      But she didn't keep me.
      Tell me about her love."

One day Annie learned she was going to have a baby. Her life changed. She made choices to help you.

Your birth mother wanted you to live. For many months you grew inside her body. The bigger you grew, the bigger she grew. Sometimes she felt fat, tired, and sick. Giving you life was more important than how she looked or felt.

Your birth mother wanted you
to have a strong body.

Before Annie became pregnant,
she loved to be with her friends.
They would eat

    candy bars,

      cookies,

        potato chips,

          and soda pop.

When Annie knew you were growing
inside her, she quit eating junk food.

No more cans of potato chips.

No bags of cookies.

Annie ate things like peas, carrots,
and tomatoes to help you grow.

When she chewed calcium tablets,
sometimes Annie gagged and
pulled faces.

But she ate the tablets again
the next day. Why? The doctor
told Annie the calcium was
good for your bones.

Your birth mother wanted you
to have a good mind. Annie didn't take
any drugs that might damage your
brain.

Even if she had a cold or a headache,
she took care of you first. How?
Annie checked with her doctor before
she took any medicine.

Say no to drugs

For Head ache

For cough

even cough medicine

Your birth mother wanted you
to be in her memory always.

Annie had an ultrasound movie
taken of you while you were
growing inside her.

She kept a copy of this video
to remind her
of the months
you lived
so close to her heart.

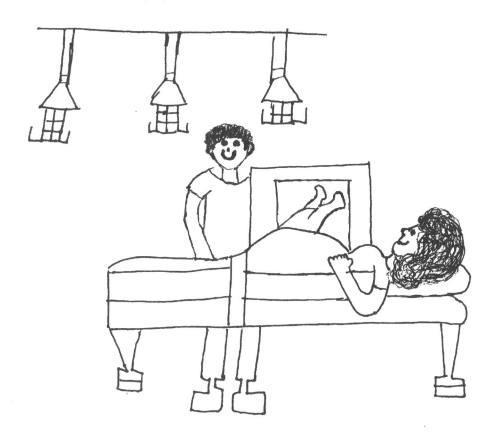
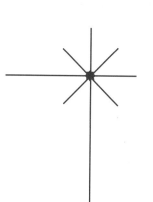

Your birth mother wanted to hold
   and hug
      and kiss you forever.

She wanted to rock you to sleep,
   kiss you awake,
      watch you grow,
         and dry your tears.

Annie knew she would be happier
   if she kept you.

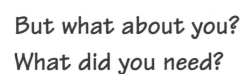

But what about you?

What did you need?

Annie read about babies born to
very young mothers...

    Mothers who were still in school...

    Mothers without jobs...

    Mothers without Fathers
      to help love and care for the children.

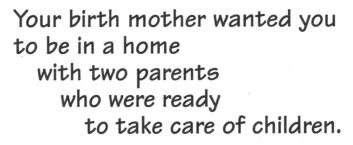

Your birth mother wanted you
to be in a home
    with two parents
        who were ready
            to take care of children.

The only way to do this
    was to let you be adopted.

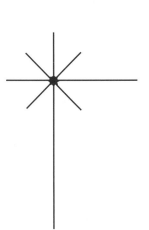

Your birth mother wants you to know
she still thinks about you often.

She especially thinks of you
  on your birthday.

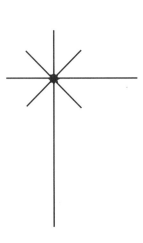

Your birth mother wants you
to know she is very happy
you are in your family.

Annie gave wonderful gifts

to you and your family.

She gave you

THE GIFT OF LIFE.

She gave your family YOU...

the child of their dreams.

Wherever you are,
Annie's Child,
She loved you
Before you were born.
She loves you now.
Never…
Never…
Never, will she stop loving you.

DEDICATED TO...

All adopted children. Somewhere, a birth mother cared enough to give each child life.

Jeff and Jackie, the precious children my husband, Jerry, and I cherish–now and forever.

The mothers that gave our children life. On a cloudless night, if our children's birth mothers look up into the vast heavens and try to count the stars, they will know of our impossibility to find enough words to express how much and how often we thank God for them, our children's first mothers.

Angel Annie. Who else but an angel could take the physical discomfort of an unexpected pregnancy, the personal guilt and social torture that accompanied the event from conception to court documents, and then turn this entire heartbreaking ordeal into a miracle for complete strangers?

The thoughts of total and final separation from the child of her womb, shattered our Annie's heart, the heart that some people said such an act would prove she did not have. Months of putting her child first in every thing she did, still did not prepare Annie for her ultimate test.

In agony, Annie reached heavenward. At last God granted her a supreme surge of strength–the strength to let go–to let her beloved child go to the desperately empty arms of complete strangers. The arms of a couple who had pleaded and bargained and begged God to bless their home with a child.

Only an angel like Annie could make such a sacrifice!

AUTHOR:

Jolene Durrant's intense love for children and her adoption experiences motivated her to capture in print this story of love. A lifelong resident of Utah, she and her husband Jerry Griffiths are the adoptive parents of two incredible children. Annie, their foster daughter, remains a cherished friend.

PHOTOGRAPHY and CONSULTANT:

Steve Allred, friend of the author and a Marriage and Family Therapist.

ILLUSTRATORS:

Adopted children ages 5 to 14: Jackie, Tiffanie, Nathan, Nicole, Kendall, Kelani, Malia, Gabriela, Amy, Kimberly, Christian, and Tyler.

ACKNOWLEDGMENTS:

I express my appreciation to those who have loved and supported me throughout my life and in the writing of this book: my husband, Jerry; my children, Jeff and Jackie; my parents, Duane and Helen Durrant; my sister, Turana; my brother, Ross; and my friends, Colleen and Helen.

Others who were there in pivotal moments guiding me to a better path: Kerry Welch, Jonee Allred, Steve Allred, Jeffrey Holland, Patricia Holland, M. Q. Rice, and Mary Krogness.

Family and friends who have shared and enriched my life's journey: Aunt Merline, Aunt LaRae, Linda Merline, Michele, Marianne, Elaine, Leslie, Pierco, Uncle George, Brook and Debi Richan.

Special thanks to those who helped in a direct way with this book: Lisa Anne Horman, whose story this is. Derek Hansen for polishing these pages until press-ready with his artistic touch, attention to details, and graphics excellence. Steve Allred's soulful encouragement and poignant photography. Linda for her insightful guidance. Grace Mann's zest, wisdom, and friendship. Eric Parkinson for many hours of work. Jan and Quincy, photographic models. The children artists, their adoptive parents, and their birth parents. Others: Laurie, Vici, Glenda, Elaine Terry, Josh Bevans, Cari Buckner, and Carolyn Aagard.